WACKY WIZARD'S HANDBOOK

John Byrne

PUFFIN BOOKS

PUFFIN BOOKS

Published by the Penguin Group
Penguin Books Ltd, 27 Wrights Lane, London W8 5TZ, England
Penguin Putnam Inc., 375 Hudson Street, New York, New York 10014, USA
Penguin Books Australia Ltd, Ringwood, Victoria, Australia
Penguin Books Canada Ltd, 10 Alcorn Avenue, Toronto, Ontario, Canada M4V 3B2
Penguin Books (NZ) Ltd, Private Bag 102902, NSMC, Auckland, New Zealand

On the World Wide Web at: www.penguin.com

Penguin Books Ltd, Registered Offices: Harmondsworth, Middlesex, England

First published 2000

1

British Library Cataloguing in Publication Data
A CIP catalogue record for this book is available from the British Library

ISBN 0-141-30928-8

Wacky Wizard School

Greetings to all Wacky Wizards, Wicked Witches, Goblins, Gremlins and Gnomes. Pass through the doorway of this, the most wacky school for wizards ever, and you'll never be the same again!

There are notions for potions, tips for tricks and enough jokes to make even the most wicked warlock wail. I can tell you're just itching to put those wizarding skills to the test — but remember, not everyone's got what it takes: a cunning brain, sleight of hand, and enough hard cash to bribe all the teachers at exam time!

Only joking ... actually, a small amount of cash will do! So, what are you waiting for? Get on your bike (or should that be broomstick?), dust off your wand and bring that toad out of retirement, and you'll be a truly wacky wizard in no time at all.

Ah ... hang on ... what's that? School inspectors on their way? Yikes — time for me to perfect my disappearing act!

Yours

Theodophilus Trickster

Head (and bottom) Teacher

— due to an unfortunate accident during a sawing-the-teacher-in-half demonstration!

WITCH HAZEL'S PROBLEM PAGE

Are you a worried wizard or a weary witch? Let me solve your problems as if by magic!

> DEAR WITCH HAZEL
> I am a very distressed teenage witch – last night I looked in my magic mirror and found a huge nasty spot on the end of my nose. What can I do?
> Embarrassed, Edinburgh

Dear Embarrassed

You poor thing, I can imagine how upset you must be having just one nasty spot on the end of your nose when any self-respecting witch should have a whole collection of spots, a couple of warts and a good selection of boils and pimples too. Try eating lots of chocs and greasy foods and not washing your face for three weeks. If you still can't manage any more spots, you can always glue on a couple of rice crispies.

MAGIC MIRROR DO YOU THINK ANYONE WILL NOTICE THIS SPOT ON MY NOSE?

OF COURSE NOT... THEY'LL BE MUCH TOO DAZED BY YOUR HORRIBLE PONGY BREATH!

DEAR WITCH HAZEL
Every time I put on my wizard's hat I get a terribly sharp headache. What could be causing this?
Agonized, Acton

Dear Agonized
Try putting your hat on with the point the other way up.

ARRGH! I'VE GOT MY HAT ON THE RIGHT WAY, BUT I'M STILL GETTING STABBING PAINS — WHAT SHOULD I DO?

STOP CARRYING YOUR PET HEDGEHOG AROUND INSIDE IT.

DEAR WITCH HAZEL
Help! I am suffering from a magic leak! My magical powers are out of control and are interfering with everything I touch! What can I do?
Dangerous, Dartmoor

Dear Dangerous
Sorry, I can't answer your letter — as soon as I opened the envelope, my pen turned into a hippopotamus.

DEAR WITCH HAZEL
Where can I get some second-hand fairy dust?
Meany, Manchester

Dear Meany
Try looking inside a fairy vacuum-cleaner

DEAR WITCH HAZEL
Just for a change I am not asking for something. Instead I am sending you a cheque for £5,000 as I heard that your pet cat recently ate your life savings. I hope this helps.
Glenda Goodwitch, Gloucester

Dear Glenda
Thanks for the cheque, but I don't really need it. It's true that my cat ate my life savings but ever since then I've had lots of money in the kitty.

DEAR WITCH HAZEL
Can you please tell us why you are writing a problem page and offering to help people with their worries, as our mum and dad have always told us that witches are horrible creatures who only want to eat little boys and girls like us.
Hansel and Gretel, The Other Side of the Forest

Dear Hansel and Gretel
Sadly, your mum and dad have fallen for the completely untrue rumour that witches are only interested in eating people. Why not visit me in my ginger-bread cottage and I shall be only too happy to put the record straight.
Your friend, Witch Hazel
P.S. Do make sure that you're both nice and plump when you come, and don't forget to have a bath in salt, vinegar and tomato ketchup beforehand

DEAR WITCH HAZEL
Gotcha! That last letter wasn't from Hansel and Gretel at all, but from us, their parents! We'll be round to the gingerbread house shortly and we won't be bringing salt, vinegar or tomato ketchup, but don't worry – we'll make sure you've had your chips!
Yours very sincerely
Winifred and Walter, the Witch-Bashing Woodcutters

DEAR WITCH HAZEL
You've got to help me! My crystal ball is on the blink and I can't see into the future any more. What can I do?
Clueless, Canterbury

Dear Clueless
Sorry, Clueless, we can't answer your letter as Witch Hazel has had to leave very suddenly, muttering something about woodcutters. (It's a shame your crystal ball isn't working or else you would have foreseen this and saved yourself a stamp.)

WIZARD WIT

Why did the wizard bring a dragon to music class?
He wanted to practise his scales.

COLD OR NO COLD, YOU'RE GOING TO HAVE TO STOP SNEEZING IF YOU DON'T LIKE SETTING FIRE TO YOUR TONGUE!

What's fat and warty and lives just outside the wizard's castle?
The Yellow Brick Toad.

"FOLLOW THE SMELL-O BRICK ROAD"

WHIFF!

Why was the wizard's bedroom full of bats?
Because he'd left the landing light on.

CAN I ¿SNUFFLE? BORROW YOUR HANKY? I'VE GOT THIS REALLY AWFUL COLD.

OH NO! IT'S THE WIZARD OF OOZE!

Why was the wizard's castle empty?
Because he'd just popped out for a spell.

What lives at the end of the Yellow
Brick Road and is covered in cement?
The Wiz-hard of Oz.

How do bats get into wizards' castles?
Through the flaps.

HELP! I'M BEING
CHASED BY
VAMPIRE DENTURES!

WHEN IT
COMES TO
BEING MONSTROUS
WE'RE IN A
"GLASS" OF OUR
OWN!

Did you hear about the very old wizard
who had vampire teeth?
They came out at night.

Lonely? Heartbroken? Depressed?

Why sit and wait for Mister or Miss Right
to hop into your life?
Contact:

DIAL-A-FROG

Choose from over 2,000 frogs, toads and other
reptiles, at least one in every 100 of which is
guaranteed to be a prince or princess under
a magical spell and awaiting transformation
by a kiss.

SPECIAL OFFER: Every hundredth customer receives a
complimentary tube of lip balm and wart-removing cream
(you'll need it after kissing the other 99 frogs).

Wacky Witches

First Witch: How is your new cat working out?
Second Witch: So fur so good.

WHY HAVE YOU GOT A HIPPOPOTAMUS ON THE END OF YOUR BROOMSTICK?

IT'S THE CAT'S DAY OFF.

Why did the witch put a watch on the end of her broomstick?
She wanted to make time fly.

Wizard School Noticeboard

Cricket bat for sale. £50 or nearest offer. (But it had better be a good price. Training the bat to play cricket took me ages.)

TRAFFIC INFORMATION:
Please try to set out for school at least half an hour early this week as traffic has been diverted due to a burst water-main in the middle of the yellow brick road.
(A hole has been dug, and the Water Board are looking into it.)

ITEMS FOUND:
Would the person who left a glass slipper behind at the annual school dance come and claim it, or we will throw it out. (And while you're at it, could you please hurry up and remove the pumpkin, rats and mice from the car park?)

FOOTBALL FIXTURES:
ALL SCHOOL FOOTBALL MATCHES HAVE BEEN CANCELLED UNTIL FURTHER NOTICE. SINCE WE STARTED USING CRYSTAL BALLS INSTEAD OF LEATHER ONES, THE LOSING TEAM CAN SEE THE RESULT IN ADVANCE AND DON'T EVEN BOTHER TO TURN UP.

Special note for pupils in fortune-telling class:

Yes, of course it's blank – if you're any good at fortune-telling you should be able to work out what it says for yourself.

PETS' DAY

Please note that for this year's pets' day pupils are more than welcome to bring in cats, frogs, snakes and unicorns as normal. However, it would be appreciated if all dragons were kept muzzled as otherwise they cause fires all over the

BLOOD DONORS: Count Vernon Von Vampyre has kindly agreed to give a talk in the school hall, on becoming 'a blood donor'. This will take place in the evening since he is nervous about attending morning assembly for some reason. However, he has promised that any pupils who attend won't miss out on their tea as he will personally make sure they all get a bite.

SCHOOL TRIP:

This year's school trip to the Bermuda Triangle has been cancelled as the group that went last year never came back.

★ ★ ★ ★ ★ ★ ★ ★ ⭐ ★ ★ ★ ★ ★ ★ ★

Wizards v Witches

Witch: How do you keep a stupid wizard in suspense?
Wizard: I don't know.
Witch: I'll tell you tomorrow.

Why did the wizard put a toad in the witch's bed?
Because he couldn't find a rat.

Witch: Why have you filled my cauldron with cornflakes?
Wizard: I'll tell you tomorrow.
Witch: Why can't you tell me now?
Wizard: Because it's a cereal.

LOOK-IF YOU DON'T STOP WAKING ME UP EVERY MORNING I'M GOING.TO TURN YOU INTO A TIN CAN!

OOER! NOW I REALLY AM AN ALARMED CLOCK!

Witch: I've lost my cat.
Wizard: Why don't you put an ad in the paper?
Witch: Don't be silly, cats can't read!

Wizard: You've been telling everyone that we wizards are a bit thick.
Witch: I'm sorry — did you want to keep it a secret?

Witch: I've got my mother's good looks.
Wizard: I'm not surprised your mother wanted to get rid of them!

Witch: You'll never be as good at magic as me!
Wizard: I hope not — I've set my sights a lot higher than that!

Coining It!

Here's a really simple trick that hardly needs any practice, yet it still brings rich rewards!

You will need: Some coins and an audience of at least four people

What the magic looks like: You spread the coins — the more the better — out on top of a table and then have yourself blindfolded. Now ask one member of the audience to pick a coin, any coin. Tell this person to examine the coin carefully to make sure it's an ordinary coin, and also so that he or she can remember which one it is. Next, tell him or her to pass the coin round to the other members of the audience, so that they can remember it too. Then get someone to put the coin back with the others and mix all the coins up and move them around.

   Then, without taking off your blindfold, you pick up the coins one by one … and amaze your audience by knowing the chosen coin as soon as you touch it!

HMMM!

How the magic is done: As long as you have at least four people in the audience this trick should work. Since the chosen coin has been handled and passed around so much, it's bound to be much warmer to the touch than the other coins, and it will be easy to spot as soon as you touch it. Pretty hot trick, eh?

Magic Menagerie

What did the witch sing when the gorilla sat on her?
'King Kong, the witch is dead.'

Why was the dragon keeper out of work?
He'd just been fired.

What do you get if you cross a witch with a pig?
A wart-hog.

What's black and furry and dresses exactly like a witch?
A copycat.

What's big, grey and wrinkly and wears a wizard's hat?
A spell-ephant.

What's big and scaly and eats witches' cats?
A fur-breathing dragon.

Which is the wimpiest animal in the wizard's menagerie?
The puny-corn.

WIZARD SCHOOL RULES

1. Running in the school corridors is not allowed.
(Flying down the corridors on a broomstick is
allowed, as long as you stick to the speed limit
of 50 kilometres an hour.)

2. Pupils must wear school uniform at all times
(although they are allowed to take off pointy hats
when approaching doorways that are less than two
metres tall).

3. Pupils are not allowed to travel backwards in
time during exams to find out the answers to
history questions.

4. Nor are they allowed to travel forward in time
to find out the answers to science questions.

IN WIZARD
SCHOOL
WE DON'T
APPROVE
OF CUTTING
UP FROGS
FOR
SCIENCE
CLASS...

PARTICULARLY
WHEN YOU'VE JUST
TURNED YOUR
TEACHER
INTO
ONE...

5. And they are expressly forbidden to read their teacher's mind during exams in order to get the answers to all the other questions.

6. Smoking is a silly habit and is not allowed anywhere in the school grounds. If your pet dragon starts to smoke, throw a bucket of water over him immediately.

7. While pupils are allowed to bring apples for their teachers, student witches in particular are reminded to make sure that these apples are not of the poisonous variety.

8. All vegetarian students should make this fact known to the dinner ladies at the beginning of term so that eye of newt and ear of bat can be left off the school menus.

9. All long hair is to be worn tied up during school hours. (Unless you are a junior wizard with a long beard, in which case tying your hair up will just mean you cover your face and won't be able to see the blackboard.)

10. All pupils must eat free jelly and ice-cream and play video games all day.

11. There must be no magical tampering with the school rules. (This goes especially for the person who changed rule number 10 from the original 'no eating in class'.)

12. Anyone disobeying these rules will be suspended from school and sent to sleep for 100 years. (And don't think you can use that as an excuse for not having your homework done when you do come back.)

Froggy Fun

What do you get if you cross a frog prince with a Polo mint?
Toad in the hole.

What is a frog prince's favourite drink?
Croak-a-cola.

Let's face it, it is some people's destiny to lead very, very boring lives. Next time you're fortune-telling for one of these sad souls, keep yourself awake with the dynamic

DIGI-BALL

The only crystal ball that not only lets you look into the future and the past, but also gives you 97 movie, music and sports channels! (Don't worry – if your client catches you tuning in to your favourite monster movie instead of forcing yourself to focus on their hopeless horoscope, simply tell them that they're going to meet a tall dark handsome stranger ... and that his name's going to be King Kong!)

Wizard School Wackiness

Wizard Teacher: I'm going to report you to the headmaster. What's your name?

Wacky Wizard: Hogsbanenightshademoonbeamspiritstonetoadwart.

Wizard Teacher: Er, I think this time I'll let you off with a warning ...

Wacky Wizard: 'Teacher, Teacher — one of the witches threw my magic wand out of the window!'

Wizard Teacher: 'Oh, stop making such a fuss — it's not that serious.'

Wacky Wizard: 'Yes it is — it was still in my back pocket at the time!'

Silly Spells

Have you heard about the wizard who crossed a vampire with a snowman?
He got frost bite.

Why did the wizard shrink his bedsheets?
He wanted to sleep tight.

Why did the wizard eat his magic candles?
He fancied some light refreshment.

Why did the wizard turn his socks into sheet music?
Because someone told him his feet were starting to hum.

Have you heard about the wizard who changed himself into an oil-well?
He was really boring.

Have you heard about the wizard who changed himself into a boiled egg?
He was a little bit cracked.

Did you hear about the wacky wizard who turned himself into a river?
Nobody could get him to leave his bed.

Hanky-panky!

Every wizard needs an amazing hanky trick to wow an audience with. (Let's just hope you're not the sort of wacky wizard for whom occasionally *washing* your hanky counts as 'an amazing trick'!)

You will need: A clean hanky, a small coin, some soap

What the magic looks like: You place the coin in the middle of the hanky, fold the hanky over and then pick it up and shake it out ... and the coin has mysteriously disappeared!

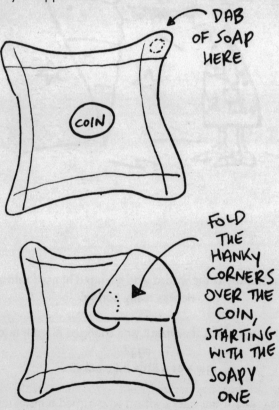

DAB OF SOAP HERE

COIN

FOLD THE HANKY CORNERS OVER THE COIN, STARTING WITH THE SOAPY ONE

How the magic is done: Before you do the trick, put a tiny piece of soap in one corner of the hanky. Make sure that this is the corner you fold over the coin first. You can ask a member of your audience to press on the coin to make sure it's still there ... actually, you are making the person press so that the coin sticks to the corner of the hanky. Lift up the hanky as shown, and the coin should end up in your hand without anyone noticing. This is a good trick to do while sitting at the table, because you can drop the coin into your lap so that it really seems to have disappeared into thin air, and your audience won't be able to sniff out the deception.

What do you call a fairy who never bathes?
Stinker Bell.

Who lives under the sea and grants wishes?
The Fairy Codmother.

What did one fortune-teller say to the other fortune-teller?
'You're fine — how am I?'

HAS SHE SEEN SOMETHING VERY SAD IN THE FUTURE?

NO...ITS JUST THAT EVERY SO OFTEN SHE LIKES TO HAVE A CRYSTAL BAWL..

WAHHH!!

Magic

Patient: 'Doctor, Doctor — I think I'm a magic wand.'
Doctor: 'How did you get in here? There's a long queue outside.'
Patient: 'The nurse waved me through.'

I'M HERE TO VISIT THE ASSISTANT I ACCIDENTALLY SAWED IN HALF..

HOSPITAL

HOW NICE — YOU'LL FIND HER UPSTAIRS IN WARDS TEN AND FOURTEEN!

Reception

What did one pack of cards say to the other pack of cards?
'I'll deal with you in a minute.'

Why aren't pixies afraid of witches and wizards?
They've done an elf defence course.

What do you find in a wacky wizard's laboratory at Christmas?
Jingle smells.

WIZARD SCHOOL DINNER MENU

Warning: Please DO NOT tell our dinner ladies that their food is fit only for animals or they may turn YOU into one.

Starter:

Soup of the Day

(please let us know in advance if you also require bread or whether you would prefer to simply soak the soup up with your wizard's beard)

Main Course:

Alphabet spaghetti (very good for spells)

Flame-grilled phoenix

(please be prepared to wait some time because every
time we put it in the flames it comes back to life again)

Bubble and Squeak

Bubble, Bubble and Squeak

Bubble, Bubble, Toil and Trouble and Squeak

Side Order:

French fries or (for students who have been turned
into frogs) French flies

MENU

SHOULD WE
HAVE A SIDE
ORDER?

I'VE
EATEN
HERE
BEFORE...
IT WOULD
BE MORE
LIKE A
SUICIDE
ORDER!

Dessert:

Fairy cakes (be sure to eat before midnight, or they turn into pumpkin pies)
Tooth fairy cakes (like fairy cakes, only sugar free)

Drinks:

Fountain of Eternal Youth (only available in children's portions)

Invisibility Potion (must be paid for in advance — we've been caught by the 'drink it and then sneak out without paying' trick too many times)

Please note:

1. We expect all dinner plates to be licked clean so you can see your face in them.

If you are a witch and your face cracks the dinner plate, an extra charge will be made.

Wacky Witches

Have you heard the joke about the witches' cauldron?
No — have you just cooked it up?

Have you heard the joke about the broomstick?
Yes, it's sweeping the country.

Who makes the witches' favourite movies?
Wart Disney.

What noise do witches make when they're flying really fast?
Broom, Broom!

What goes 'Moorb, Moorb'?
A witch flying really fast in the opposite direction.

When do witches have holes in their middles?
When it's Hollow-ween.

Why did the witch keep her cat in a fish tank?
Because she really wanted a Purr-anha.

Wizard Wit

What do wizards write on postcards?
Witch you were here.

WHY NOT SAVE YOUR STAMP? HE ALREADY KNOWS WHAT YOUR LETTER SAYS BEFORE YOU POST IT.

WIZARD'S POSTBOX

Why did the wizard pick his lottery numbers with a broomstick?
He wanted to get witch quick.

DO YOU HAVE MYSTIC POWERS?

Test yourself with this handy quiz.

1. Since you were very small have you felt great power surging through your fingertips?
(a) Yes.
(b) No.
(c) Yes — but now I know better than to stick my hand into the electricity socket.

2. Do you often have visions of the future?
(a) No.
(b) I knew you'd ask me that.

WHY ARE YOU LOOKING IN THAT GARDENING MAGAZINE?

I WANT TO SEE THE FUCHSIA...

3. Do you find that the right answer to any question is always clear to you?
(a) Yes.
(b) Yes.

4. Do you use your broomstick more often for sweeping or flying?
(a) Sweeping.
(b) Flying.
(c) So that's why I've been having trouble answering these questions. Hang on till I get rid of this broomstick and try writing with a pencil.

5. Why do you wear a tall, pointy hat?
(a) Because all wizards wear tall, pointy hats.
(b) Because all witches wear tall, pointy hats.
(c) Because I've got a tall, pointy head.

6. What's your favourite magic book?
(a) *Ye Bigge Booke of Forbidden Spelles.*
(b) *Ye Even Bigger Booke of Forbidden Spelles.*
(c) My homework notebook ... it must be a magic book because every time open it I feel like disappearing!

. When someone tells you to follow the Yellow Brick Road, do you say:

a) 'What's the Yellow Brick Road?'

b) 'Where's the Yellow Brick Road?'

c) 'How can I follow the Yellow Brick Road — it never wins any football matches.'

nd most importantly of all ...

. Do you promise never ever to reveal the secrets of wizardry to outsiders?

a) Yes.

b) No.

c) Can't tell you — it's a secret.

HECK YOUR ANSWERS: Oh, come off it — if you're a *real* wizard you'll have nagically made sure you got all the right answers in the first place.

Wizards
v
Witches

Wizard: I learned today that words can be very hurtful.
Wizard's mum: Why? Has that rotten witch been insulting you again?
Wizard: No — she dropped a big heavy magic book on my foot!

Wizard: I used to dislike witches until I got to know you.
Witch: And now you feel differently?
Wizard: Yes, now I *really* can't stand them.

Wizard: When I finish wizard school I'm going to have letters after my name.
Witch: Yes: D–A–F–T.

Wizard: I think all this fighting is just because we have different talents.
Witch: What do you mean?
Wizard: I'm talented and you're different.

Witch: I have to admit that you're a wizard of rare magical ability.
Wizard: You really mean that?
Witch: Yes — you rarely show any magical ability at all.

Wizard: My magic skills are in great shape!
Witch: They certainly should be — they've hardly ever been used.

Wizard: Can you do a spell to cure my hiccups?
Witch: No.
Wizard: Doesn't matter anyway — your face has already done the job.

Witch: I'll have you know we witches have been around since the Dark Ages!
Wizard: I'm not surprised — you look really terrible in the light.

Magic Menagerie

Did you hear about the wizard who crossed a turkey with a dragon?
He got gobble, gobble, gobbled.

IF there are DRAGONS AROUND HERE, I'M OFF BEFORE I BECOME A ROAST TURKEY!

Where do you find wizard snails?
In wizards' DIY boxes.

YOU CAN ALWAYS TELL WIZARD SNAILS - WHY LIVE IN A SHELL WHEN YOU CAN TURN IT INTO SOMETHING MUCH NICER!

ACTION WIZARD!

THE THIRTY-CENTIMETRE FIGURE
WITH REAL MAGICAL POWERS!

Don't worry about having to fiddle with buttons or batteries – this amazing figure performs lots of fantastic tricks through the power of real magic, and you don't even have to spend money on other outfits or accessories ... Action Wizard can create all this stuff magically by itself!

DON'T DELAY – SEND US YOUR MONEY TODAY!

We have received several complaints from people who have not delayed and have sent their money today — only to receive an empty box back in the post. We are very upset to be accused of being a gang of crooks — obviously it only *looks* like an empty box. In actual fact, Action Wizard is merely demonstrating his amazing powers of invisibility. In fact, you're lucky we haven't charged you extra, so there!

★ ★ ★ ★ ★ ★ ★ ★ ★ ★ 43 ★ ★ ★ ★ ★ ★ ★ ★ ★ ★

Froggy Fun

What do you wish a frog prince on his birthday?
Many hoppy returns.

'Doctor, Doctor, I've been turned into a frog!'
'Then you'll have to have a hop-peration.'

Have you heard about the singer who was turned into a frog?
Now he's the Phantom of the Hopera.

Why did the frog prince complain in the restaurant?
Because there wasn't a fly in his soup.

Where do frog princes go to get glasses?
The hoptician.

What do you get if you cross a bird with a frog prince?
Pigeon toad.

What do you say to a prince who's been turned into a frog?
Toad you so.

HAT TRICKS

Even wizards can't make old hats disappear into thin air. So get your head round these handy recycling suggestions:

1. Traffic cone for a broken-down broomstick

2. Icing flute

3. Seesaw pivot

4. Bird mask for fancy-dress party

OUCH!

JAB!

. Classroom joke to play on teacher

YUM!

6. Ice-cream cone

PRESTO!!

. Loudspeaker

8. Place to hide under when the Chief Wizard discovers you've been messing about with his hat collection.

OOER!

Wizard School Wackiness

Why did the witch bring her broomstick to wizard school?
She wanted to brush up on her magic skills.

Wizard Teacher: Who invented fairy dust?
Wizard Pupil: I don't know ... but sneeze a jolly good fellow.

Trainee Witch: When do we start doing driving lessons?
Wizard Teacher: What's that got to do with magic?
Trainee Witch: I want to turn a car into a road.

Wizard Teacher: Would you rather a witch put a spell on you or a wizard?
Wizard Pupil: I'd rather she put the spell on the wizard.

What happens at Wizard School just after invisibility class?
There's a trans-parent teacher meeting.

Why did the vampire go to Wizard School?
To study for his blood test.

What happened to the wacky wizard who was caught making noise in the school library?
They threw the book at him.

Handy Hocus Pocus!

At last a sleight-of-hand trick that works even if you're all fingers and thumbs

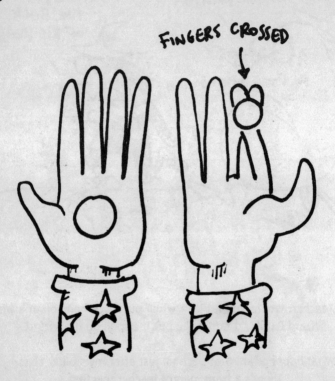

FINGERS CROSSED

You will need: Two coins, your hands

What the magic looks like: You place one coin on each hand and then turn your hands palms down on the table. When you lift your right hand, the coin that should be underneath has magically disappeared, only to reappear under your left hand!

How the magic is done: As long as you place the coins as shown, this trick really works by itself. Lay your hands, palms up, on the table, about twenty centimetres apart. Put one coin on the palm of your left hand and the other on the first and second fingers of your right hand, crossed as shown. Now, simply turn your hands over without lifting them off the table, and the coin in your right hand will be automatically thrown into your left hand faster than the eye can see. But don't take our word for it — practise a few times and see (or don't see) for yourself!

Silly Spells

Heard about the wizard who turned himself into a clock?
He was cuckoo.

Did you hear about the wizard who turned himself into an alarm clock?
It was just a wind-up.

Why spend hours on a stormy windswept hill stirring a cauldron, only to end up with a disgusting, foul-smelling brew?

Try the new

MICROWITCH

and you can have a foul-smelling brew in seconds.

This electronic device has been designed to cook all your favourite ingredients to perfection, from eye of newt to lizard's gizzard. And, should they happen to pass by your gingerbread cottage at lunchtime, it's big enough to fit both Hansel and Gretel inside.

The MICROWITCH has several popular settings which can be changed at the touch of a button:

Low power:
for nasty,
evil-smelling concoctions
High power: for evil,
nasty-smelling concoctions
Maximum power:
for school dinners

Microwitch is guaranteed to be easy and convenient to use — or at least as easy and convenient as it can be trying to find a power point on a stormy windswept hill.

Mad Magic

Did you hear about the wizard who filled his hat with cement?
He was a blockhead.

What hangs around the Yellow Brick Road and threatens people?
The Wizard of Yob.

What does Merlin the Magician wear to bed?
The nighties of the round table.

Why do fairy godmothers make good football coaches?
They always help you get to the ball.

Did you hear about the dusty magic mirror?
It was a poor reflection on its owner.

YE MAGIC MIRROR SHOPPE.

GONE TO POLISH OFF LUNCH

What's rude, smelly and comes out at night?
A foul moon.

Why do wizards like performing magic for skeletons?
Because it's always a rattling good show.

Why do wizards hate performing magic for ghosts?
Because they always go BOO!

Did you hear about the witch who parked her broomstick on a double yellow line?
She had a brush with the law.

How does a witch go to a wedding?
On her groomstick.

Wizard Wit

What wears a pointed hat and is very fast?
A whizzard.

What did the lawyers sing as they danced up the Yellow Brick Road?
'We're off to sue the Wizard.'

Get Ready!

s a special free gift to our loyal readers, we have arranged for the next bit
f the *Wacky Wizard's Handbook* to be printed on special magical paper.
imply rub this special magical star, and when you turn the page you will
nmediately be able to see into the future!

★ ★ ★ ★ ★ ★ ★ ★ ★ ★ ★ ★ ★ ★ ★ ★ ★ ★

THE
URE

Wacky Witches

Why did the witch bring her broomstick on her first date?
She wanted to sweep her date off his feet.

What did Hansel and Gretel say when the witch turned them into salad?
'Lettuce go!'

Why do all witches wear the same type of hat?
So you can't tell witch is witch.

Why do witches change people into frogs?
Because if they changed people into gorillas, the gorillas might thump them

GRR! SOME ROTTEN WIZARD'S MADE MY HEADGEAR TEN SIZES TOO LARGE!

IF I WAS YOU I'D KEEP THAT UNDER MY HAT!

Where does a witch refuel her broomstick?
At a petrol pump-kin.

Why didn't the witch get a part in the horror movie?
She failed the scream test.

What did the horror movie producers say when the witch failed the test?
'Don't cauldron us, we'll cauldron you!'

What do you get if you cross a witch with a breakfast cereal?
Snap, cackle and pop.

Magic Words by Ali Kazam

House-Training Your Witch's Cat by Kitty Litter

Under Your Spell by B. Witched

Dangerous Potions by X. Plosion

Wizards v Witches

Witch: Would you mind standing in my cauldron?
Wizard: Why?
Witch: Because this potion is supposed to have weeds in it.

Witch: When it comes to magic, I'm way out in front of you!
Wizard: I don't mind — it saves me having to look at your face!

Wizard: We wizards can do whatever we like.
Witch: You mean you *like* being stupid?

★ ★ ★ ★ ★ ★ ★ ★ ★ ★ ★ ★ ★ ★ ★

Witch: Are you accusing me of acting stupid?
Wizard: I never said you were acting.

Wizard: I always say exactly what's on my mind.
Witch: I'm surprised you say anything at all then.

Witch: I'm getting homesick at Wizard School.
Wizard: So why don't you go home? We're all sick of you.

Wizard: If you don't stop insulting me, I'd hate to be in your shoes.
Witch: I'd hate to be in your shoes, too — I know what your feet smell like.

Witch: What I say goes.
Wizard: Say your own name then!

Magic Menagerie

WHAT DO DRAGONS ORDER IN FAST FOOD JOINTS?

OUCH! DRAGON FRIES!

What do you get when you cross Naomi Campbell with a dragon?
A scale model.

What do dragons wear to Wizard School?
Blazers.

Stunt Rabbit For Hire!

Let's face it, not every magic trick goes exactly according to plan. You know it, I know it – but there's no reason for the *audience* to know it … at least, there isn't if you hire me, Seymour Stunt Rabbit, as part of your act. Unlike an ordinary bunny, I am a professional escapologist and can escape with ease from even the smallest top hat. I can also pick your volunteer's pocket and replace the card they actually picked with the one you *think* they picked. And, as for problems with the famous 'cutting the bunny in half' trick – well, I'm an expert at escaping by a hare's breadth! So remember: when your tricks go all funny, send for the bunny!

P.S. I am available for work all this year – except for this summer, when I shall be appearing as a stunt rabbit in the latest episode of the *Star Warrens* trilogy.

★ ★ ★ ★ ★ ★ ★ ★ ★ ★ ★ ★ ★ ★ ★ ★ ★ ★

Froggy Fun

WHAT TV SHOW DO
FROG PRINCES GO ON
TO TALK ABOUT THEIR
TROUBLES?

HOP-RAH
WINFREY!

What do you call a spy who's been turned into a frog?
James Pond.

What did the frog prince say to the frog princess?
Want to come back to my pad?

Where do frog princes keep their money?
In the riverbank.

Where do princes who have been turned into reptiles go to be
changed back?
To the Lizard of Oz.

When do most princes get turned into frogs?
Leap year.

Did you hear about the frog prince who was covered in dots and dashes?
He was really a morse toad.

Why was the frog hoarse?
He had a prince in his throat.

What do you call a frog prince in a kilt?
Hop scotch.

Where do frog princes change into their kilts?
In the croakroom.

ALL FINGERS AND THUMBS?

'Off with his head!' shouts the king as yet another wacky wizard trick goes wrong. But does a wacky wizard panic? Of course not — why be afraid of having your head cut off when you can pull your thumb off all by yourself?

You will need: Your hand

MAGICIAN PULLS THUMB OFF

AUDIENCE FAINTS

What the magic looks like: You grab hold of your thumb and tug it with a bit of grunting and groaning to make the whole thing look more realistic. Then, with one quick motion, you pull your thumb off and then put it back again, just in time to rush to the assistance of any audience members who may have fainted.

How the magic is done: Simply follow the steps below and remember that the trick works only if the audience are watching you face on, so be careful where you stand. (Mind you, it's never wise for wacky wizards to let the audience get between them and the door in the first place.)

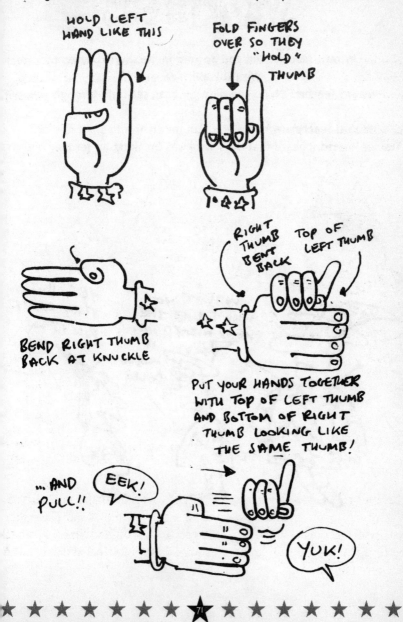

HOLD LEFT HAND LIKE THIS

FOLD FINGERS OVER SO THEY "HOLD" THUMB

BEND RIGHT THUMB BACK AT KNUCKLE

RIGHT THUMB BENT BACK

TOP OF LEFT THUMB

PUT YOUR HANDS TOGETHER WITH TOP OF LEFT THUMB AND BOTTOM OF RIGHT THUMB LOOKING LIKE THE SAME THUMB!

... AND PULL!!

EEK!

YUK!

Wizard School Wackiness

Wizard Teacher: Did you do your invisibility homework?
Wizard Pupil: Yes, sir!
Wizard Teacher: Oh no you didn't — I can see right through you.

Wizard Teacher: Why did you turn my chair into a pot of glue?
Trainee Wizard: I heard that the school was breaking up for the holidays.

Why did the witch cover her broomstick with herbs?
She wanted to get to school on thyme.

How do dragons wake up for Wizard School?
They set the fire alarm.

Wizard Teacher: Why are you carrying that pot of paint and that step ladder?

Wizard Pupil: Because for homework you told us we had to write an essay on a dragon.

What's the most difficult subject at Wizard School?
Mathi-magics.

Which is the smallest classroom in Wizard School?
The one for Gnome Economics.

SEEING STARS!

Wizards place a lot of faith in horoscopes, so perhaps you should check out your audience's star signs before your own wizardry goes horribly wrong.

SAGITTARIUS

Careful! Even if they can't work out how your tricks are done, they may take a shot in the dark.

CAPRICORN

You needn't expect Capricorneans to concentrate on your tricks — they're always too busy acting the goat.

AQUARIUS

They're liable to pour cold water on any magic you try to do.

PISCES

No matter how well you practise your tricks, they're bound to suspect something fishy.

ARIES

t's no fun doing magic for Ariens — it's just too easy to pull the wool over their eyes.

TAURUS

Trying to perform magic in front of Taureans is like a red rag to a bull.

WE CAN WORK OUT ALL YOUR TRICKS...

AFTER ALL — TWO HEADS ARE BETTER THAN ONE.

GEMINI

Don't perform for Geminians unless you fancy doing the same trick twice.

CANCER

Don't expect any rewards if you're doing your tricks for Cancerians — they've always been a little shellfish.

LEO

Be careful about trying tricks on Leoians — they may roar with approval, b them might also bite your head off.

VIRGO

By now you may be virgin' on a decision not to do your tricks for any star sign at all!

LIBRA

And on balance you could be right.

SCORPIO

...f course, since horoscopes are a load of old rubbish anyway, you might as ...ell stop wasting your time reading this page and go and do your tricks for anyone you like.

...ow's that for a sting in the tail?)

Silly Spells

Why did the wizard turn himself into a slice of bread?
He wanted to spend time loafing around.

Have you heard about the wizard who turned himself into
Father Christmas?
He got the sack.

Why did the wizard drop his playing cards in the mud?
So he could try some dirty tricks.

Did you hear about the wizard who turned himself into a fruit bowl?
He was bananas.

CRUMBS! IT'S
WIZARD BREAD!!

I'M GOING
TO USE MY
LOAF AND
GET OUT OF
HERE!

Did you hear about the wizard who turned himself into an apple tree?
People started picking on him.

Have you heard about the wizard who turned himself into a bridge?
He didn't know what came over him.

Did you hear about the wizard who turned himself into a cash register?
The change did him good.

What happened to the prince's car after he was turned into a frog?
It got toad away.

Have you heard about the wizard who gave himself an extra head?
He immediately had second thoughts.

INVISIBILITY POTION

Being able to disappear at will is one of a wizard's most important skills but, as you know, it takes a huge amount of magical effort to make this spell work. Now you can disappear the lazy way with our super-strength invisibility potion. Just one swig from this bottle and you are guaranteed to be made totally and completely invisible for as long as you want!

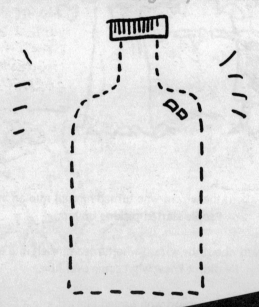

STOP PRESS!

Sorry – this product is no longer available, due to supply problems. We have lots of bottles of the potion left, but we just can't find them at the moment – they are invisible, after all!

MAD MAGIC

What do you get if you cross a witch with a ton of dynamite?
A boomstick.

Why do witches and wizards never take their hats off at the disco?
They want to dance peak to peak.

'Doctor, Doctor, I've turned into a witch's cat.'
'You must be kitten!'

Magic Menagerie

Why are bats lazy?
Because all they do is hang around all day.

Why should you never do magic tricks for stick insects?
Because they always twig.

What do you get if you cross a dragon with a dentist?
Fire drill.

Why could none of the animals on Noah's Ark play card tricks?
Because Noah stood on the deck.

What do you do if a wicked witch with a large hat sits in front of you in the cinema?
Miss the film.

What's the best way to hire a wizard?
Make him stand on a box.

Are you a wobbly wizard or a saggy sorcerer? Solve your weight problems with our

Wizard Workout

1. Swing arms to the left.

2. Swing arms to the righ

3. Swing arms to the left.

4. Swing arms to the righ

5. Realize you should have let go of your magic wand before you started swinging your arms about.

SHAZAM!!!

6. Realize you've accidentally turned yourself into a large pink elephant.

7. Realize that elephants are *supposed* to be fat, tuck into a large plate of currant buns, and relax.

Wizard Wit

What goes all around the wizard's castle but never moves?
The moat.

What did one invisible wizard say to the other invisible wizard?
'It's nice not to see you again.'

What do you give an angry wizard?
Plenty of room!

What do wizards become after they are two hundred years old?
Two hundred and one years old.

'Have you heard about the wizard who made his own nose disappear?'
'No — how did he smell?'
'Terrible.'

Which hand do wizards use to stir their potions?
Neither — they use a spoon.

What's the wizards' favourite dance?
The Loco-potion.

STICKY TRICK

Here's a trick that will definitely get you a big hand!

You will need: A magic wand (or a pen), your hand

What the magic looks like: You place your hand over your magic wand and lift it from the table. The wand magically sticks to your hand!

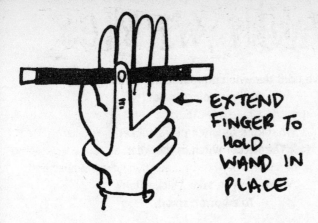

← EXTEND
FINGER TO
HOLD
WAND IN
PLACE

MAKE SURE
YOU DON'T SHOW
THE UNDERSIDE
OF YOUR HAND
OR GLORY COULD
SLIP THROUGH
YOUR FINGERS!

How the magic is done: This is one of those tricks that look ridiculously simple when you know how it is done — but it looks quite mysterious to an audience who don't. All you do is place your hand, palm down, over the wand, with your other hand gripping your wrist, as shown. Note that the first finger of the gripping hand is tucked underneath the hand that is covering the wand. Start to lift the wand, using your thumb to hold it in place, and, as you keep talking, secretly extend your hidden finger to press the wand against your palm. Now you can take your thumb away, and the wand will look as if it is held in place by magic!

Wacky Witches

Why did the witch jump into her cauldron?
She was going to pot.

What kind of witch plays cricket?
The Wicket Witch of the West.

Where do you take a sick witch?
To a horror-spital.

What do witches get on their birthdays?
Older.

WHAT DOES IT SAY ON A WITCH'S GREETING CARD?

"HAGGY BIRTHDAY TO YOU!"

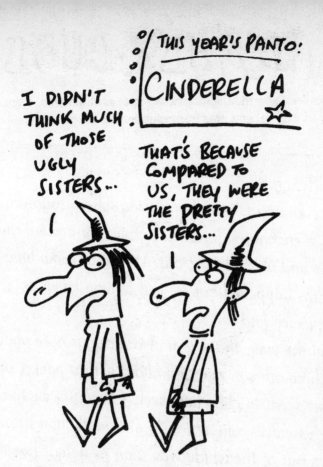

Did you hear about the witch who turned herself into a pair of glass slippers?
Yes — she was a real pane.

Why do witches fly around on broomsticks?
Because vacuum cleaners are much too heavy.

Why did the witch stop telling fortunes?
She couldn't see any future in it.

What does the witch hang on her washing line?
Her abracadab-bras.

HANDY HEX-CUSES!

Whether you're a wizard, a human or any species in between, there's nothing nearly as magical as a note from your parents for getting you out of trouble!

Dear Teacher

Please excuse our son for missing school today, as a huge enchanted forest has grown up around our castle and we can't get out. We don't know how this has happened but we will let you know as soon as we find out.

By the way, thank you also for your note about catching our son mucking about with a packet of magic seeds in class last week. Obviously we treated this matter very seriously and made him throw them out of the window as soon as he got home.

Mr and Mrs Wizard

Dear Teacher
I am writing to complain about our daughter Wanda Witch being bullied in school. Every time the school bell goes 'Ding, dong' the other pupils shout 'The witch is dead', which is very upsetting for Wanda as she is very much alive ... unlike her Uncle Vernon the Vampire, who has promised that you are going to get it in the neck if you don't sort this problem out, sharpish.
Mr and Mrs Hagg

Dear Teacher
Could you please stop giving our daughter Tina the Tooth Fairy so much homework as she has long since collected all the broken and fallen-out teeth in our family and has now started nicking perfectly good teeth while we are asleep. We are starting to feel that we have bitten off more than we can chew ... in fact since Tina has left us with no teeth we can't chew very much at all. We know that a wise and wonderful wizard teacher like you will be able to help us (hope you don't think we're sucking up to you).

Mr and Mrs Molar

Dear Teacher
Sorry it's taken so long to reply to the letter you wrote us about our son Merlin. The silly boy stuck our letter-opener into a stone and couldn't get it out until his mate Arthur came around to help him.
Mr and Mrs Roundtable

SO, MERLIN — WHERE DID YOU TRAIN TO WORK WITH KING ARTHUR?

I WENT TO KNIGH SCHO

Dear Teacher
We are sorry that our son has been copying from other pupils. He is very proud of his shape-shifting skills and likes to practise them whenever he can, but we do understand that transforming himself into an exact double of the pupil sitting next to him is likely to cause you a lot of confusion, and we promise it will never happen again.
Mr and Mrs Changeling

Dear Teacher
Thank you for your letter telling us how our daughter Winifred is the nicest, sweetest, best-behaved pupil in the school. We have explained to her that this is not how a wicked witch is supposed to behave, and she has promised to try and do much better ... er, worse, in future.
Mr and Mrs Wicked Witch of the West

Magic Menagerie

What do you get if you cross a wizard with a cow?
A moo-gician.

What do you get if you cross a cat and a dragon?
Blackened crispy mice.

What race game do dragons play?
Scale-ectric.

Why are kangaroos good at magic?
Because they can hide lots of things in their pockets.

WHAT'S THE BEST DAY TO TAKE YOUR DRAGON FOR A WALK?

OUCH! FRY-DAY!!

SIZZLE

Why do chickens do magic?
For their own hen-tertainment.

What do you get if you cross a dragon with a football team?
Queens Spark Rangers.

What's brown and flaky and breathes fire?
Puff Pastry the Magic Dragon.

Why should you never do magic for skunks?
Because when they catch you cheating they kick up a stink.

Wizards v Witches

Wizard: What would you say if I told you wizards were much better than witches at magic?

Witch: I wouldn't say anything — it's hard to talk and laugh at the same time.

WHAT DO YOU CALL A WIZARD WHO FALLS INTO A CAULDRON?

STEW-PID!

Witch: Hey! Are you spitting into my cauldron?

Wizard: No — but I'm getting closer every time.

DIAL-A-TALL-DARK-STRANGER

Hi, I'm Sid Stranger. I am very tall and very dark and I am available at very reasonable rates* to hang about outside your fortune-telling booth so that, just as you predicted, I will be the first person your customer meets when they come outside.

24-hour emergency service

* Please note: If, as usually happens, I get arrested for loitering, my bail money will be added to your fee.

Mad Magic

Which fairy always has indigestion?
The goblin.

Why do wizards have pointed hats on their heads?
Because if they had wellington boots on their heads they'd look silly.

Did you hear about the comedian who let a magician saw him in two?
He was a half wit.

What do dragons do before taking flight?
They check their wing mirrors.

What did the dragon do at the wedding?
It toasted the bride and groom.

What do you get if you cross a wizard with a lemon?
A sour-cerer.

Why are pigs no good at card tricks?
Because they are ham-fisted.

Why did the wizard jump up and down after drinking his magic potion?
Because he'd forgotten to shake the bottle first.

The Magic Mirror

All the latest news from the world of wizardry.

FEARSOME FOLIAGE FLATTENS FINE FELLOW

Wizard Windy's attempt to raise money for charity by sitting in a bath full of baked beans has had to be cancelled when it was discovered that the bath had accidentally been filled with magic beans instead of baked beans.

Suddenly finding himself on top of a 120-metre-high beanstalk, Wizard Windy immediately set a new charity record: for the world's longest bungee jump without a rope.

ARABIAN KNIGHTS CALL IT A DAY

The genie of the lamp and his master, Aladdin, today announced that their successful business partnership had come to an end. They refused to comment on the reason for the split, but it is rumoured that the genie got tired of Aladdin rubbing him up the wrong way.

FAIRY FOUL PLAY FOILED BY FURRY FELONS

A fairy godmother was today helping police with their inquiries after the theft of a luxury limousine from outside the royal palace. 'I promised Cinderella that she would arrive at the palace ball in style,' Ms Glenda Goodness declared. 'But is it my fault that those greedy ugly sisters had scoffed all the available pumpkins? What choice did I have but to break into the Prince's limo with the aid of a leftover coat-hanger from Cinders' dress, and then nick it? I would have got away with it, too, if those magical coachmen hadn't snitched on me. But then, they always were a pair of dirty rats.'

BABE BORNE AWAY BY BRAND-NEW BROOMSTICK

The new XL4 turbo-powered broomstick was launched at the Motor Show yesterday. Unfortunately, supermodelwitch Naomi Grumble had forgotten to let go of the broomstick before it was launched and took off at 00 mph. However, she seems to have enjoyed the journey, and she telephoned s to say she was over the moon.

WITCH WRUFFED UP BY WILD WOOFER

Our picture shows Witch Wendy recovering in hospital after kissing a frog that she had been told was actually a prince. And it was ... Prince, the large angry Rottweiler dog, that is.

Wizard Wit

Wizard: Doctor, Doctor, my beard keeps falling out — can you give me something to keep it in?

Doctor: Certainly — what about this little paper bag?

Why was the wizard's beard all sticky?
Because he was using a honeycomb.

What do you call a dead sorcerer?
'The Wizard of Was.'

Why did the wizard stir himself into his magic potion?
Because people were always telling him that he should learn to be a better mixer.

Why did the wizard turn himself into a tree?
So he could turn over a new leaf.

Did you hear about the wizard who turned himself into a dustbin?
Yes — but I thought it was a load of rubbish.

Wizard: Doctor, Doctor, every time I put my Wizard School blazer on, I get a terrible pain in my eye.
Doctor: Maybe you should take your magic wand out of your top pocket.

Any old wizard can make objects fly around the room — here's how you can go one better by not only making objects fly, but having them magically link up in mid-air too.

You will need: A bank note (don't worry — if you're a particularly impoverished wizard, a piece of paper cut to the same size as a banknote will do), two paper clips

What the magic looks like: You clip two paperclips on to a banknote as shown and give it a sharp tug at both ends. Hey presto, the clips will fly into the air and magically link together.

PUT ONE CLIP HERE...
AND THE OTHER HERE SO THE NOTE IS IN A 'Z' SHAPE!

Marvellous!

WITH TRICKS
LIKE THIS
YOUR WIZARD
CAREER
SHOULD REALLY
TAKE OFF!

LINK!

TUG

TUG

How the magic is done: Er ... it just is ... OK?!

Wizards v Witches

Wizard: I'm worried about getting close to you — I might get a big wart on the end of my nose!
Witch: You've already got one ... Oh, sorry, that's just your face.

Witch: Are you trying to make me look foolish?
Wizard: I don't have to — you do a really good job all by yourself.

First Witch: I really hate wizards.
Second Witch: Well, just eat the chips, then.

Wizard: Do you know what masters of magic eat for breakfast?
Witch: No.
Wizard: I didn't think you would.

Witch: Can you help me boil the water in my cauldron?
Wizard: Why should I?
Witch: Because you're usually so good at getting people steamed up.

Wizard: This place isn't big enough for both of us!
Witch: Good luck with your fish-free diet, then!

Witch: You'd look so much better if you combed your beard differently.
Wizard: How should I comb it?
Witch: How about over your face?

ALL I DID WAS TRY
TO SELL YOU A PIE
AND YOU TURNED ME
INTO A WART ON THE
END OF YOUR NOSE!

OH, BE QUIET,
PIMPLE
SIMON!

Wacky Witches

Did you hear about the witch who always did her magic while still in bed?
Her doctor had told her to lie down for a spell!

Why did the witch turn herself into a magnet?
She wanted to make herself more attractive.

If you're a proper witch, the importance of having a black cat is not to be sneezed at … or at least it's not unless you're one of the growing number of witches who are allergic to cats.

Let's face it, you're hardly likely to strike fear into anyone's heart by flying through the air with a tortoise, a goldfish or even a pet rock on the end of your broomstick. But you won't look too good with a red runny nose either (after all, everyone knows witches are supposed to have green runny noses).

The solution? Try our specially knitted

CAT COSY

Simply pop this specially designed cosy over your cat and you can go about your evil work without a single scratch or sniff.

Of course we can't guarantee that you won't get lots of scratches when you finally take the cat cosy off your maddened moggie.

Wizard School Wackiness

Wizard Teacher: You are the greatest waste of space I have ever seen.
Trainee Witch: Oh goody!
Wizard Teacher: What do you mean 'Goody'?
Trainee Witch: It's the first time I've ever been great at anything!

Wizard Teacher: Why have you turned that bunny into a frog?
Wizard Pupil: Because you told us to pull a ribbit out of our hats.

Wizard Pupil: Every time I do magic, I see spots before my eyes.
Wizard Teacher: Have you seen a doctor?
Wizard Pupil: No — just spots.

Trainee Witch: I never done my magic homework.

Wizard Teacher: I *haven't* done my magic homework.

Trainee Witch: Oh good — if you never done it either, there's no need for me to worry.

First Wizard Pupil: Why have you changed yourself into a boa constrictor?

Second Wizard Pupil: Because I've got a terrible crush on my teacher.

Wizard Teacher: Why have you turned the school computer into a big savage dog?

Wizard Pupil: I wanted to see if its bark would be worse than its byte.

Wizard Teacher: I thought I told you to write an essay on mind-reading.

Wizard Pupil: I did, sir.

Wizard Teacher: So how come you've given me three blank pages?

Wizard Pupil: I decided to use your mind as an example.

I GOT MY WITCH
KICKED OUT OF THE
WIZARD SCHOOL
COMPUTER CLASS-
I SWALLOWED
THE MOUSE!

What are you planning to do when you leave Wizard School? No, we mean besides breathing a sigh of relief? If you're still not sure how best to use your magic powers, take a look at these exclusive interviews with all the top magic movers and shakers ...

The *Wacky Wizard Handbook*

COSMIC CAREERS GUIDE

OCCUPATION: WIZARD

What's your name?

Merlin Magick.

Did you spend long at Wizard School learning your job?

I'm afraid I dropped out of Wizard School. It's a very painful memory.

It shouldn't be all that painful ... a lot of successful people have dropped out of school.

Yes, but with Wizard School being halfway up a mountain, it was a 3,500-metre drop.

MERLIN MAGICK

Why did you drop out?

Actually, I was thrown out for sewing pictures of stars on to my costume.

But all wizards have pictures of stars on their costumes.

Yes, but the stars I sewed on were Bruce Willis, Leonardo DiCaprio and Arnold Schwarzenegger.

How come you're not wearing your wizard's hat?

Because I accidentally chopped the top off it when I was sticking a sword into a stone yesterday.

And now you can't wear it?

Of course not – it would be pointless.

Any advice you'd give to someone starting Wizard School today?

Yes – work hard, practise your spelling and crawl around on your hands and knees all day long.

Why crawl around on your hands and knees?

Because you might find the piece of chewing gum I dropped while I was there and you could send it back to me.

OCCUPATION: WITCH

What's your name?

Wendolyn Wickedd.

Would you say that witches are usually good-natured, sweet-tempered and very, very beautiful or old, ugly and very evil?

That depends.

Depends on what?

On whether you'd like to spend the rest of your life as an interviewer or as a particularly warty toad.

Ahem ... Now that we've established that witches are *always* good-natured, sweet-tempered and beautiful, how do you manage to keep your good looks?

WENDOLYN WICKEDD

Well, I spend a lot of my time relaxing on the beach. In fact I'm not so much a wicked witch as a sandwitch.

We hear you've been taking acting lessons recently ...

That's right – so now I'm a ham sandwitch.

You must let us know next time you're in a play — we can print a photo in the *Wacky Wizard's Handbook.*

Wouldn't that make me a ham and 'cheese' sandwitch? And anyway I can't have my photograph taken now – you lot have kept me talking on the beach for so long I've got really badly sunburned!

Hey! That means you're now a toasted ham and cheese sandwitch.

Right! That's it — It's toad time!

Oo-er! Looks like we'd better hop it!

OCCUPATION: FAIRY GODMOTHER

What's your name?

Tilly Twinkletoes.

What other names are you known by?

The Good Fairy, the Kindly Fairy, the Blue Fairy.

Why the Blue Fairy?

You try flying around in this weather dressed in just this little spangly dress.

Why do you always give everyone three wishes?

Because if I gave everyone three fishes, there'd be a terrible smell.

Why don't any of your spells last past midnight?

They could do, but nobody wants to pay me overtime.

You mean, fairies have to get paid for what they do?

Of course we do. Why do you think I spend all Christmas sitting on top of a prickly fir tree?

So that's your main place of work?

No, it's just one of my many branches.

Tilly Twinkletoes

If you need money so badly, why not become a tooth fairy?

I don't think I'd enjoy that – I'd always be down in the mouth.

OCCUPATION: GNOME

What's your name?
You've got to guess.
Er ... Rumpelstiltskin.
Arrgh! It's not fair! Ever since those stupid Brothers Grimm wrote that fairy tale, everybody knows my name! If I ever get hold of them, I'll make life pretty Grimm for them, I can tell you!

Rumpleskiltskin

Doesn't it bother you being the bad guy in all those fairy stories?
Of course not – everyone remembers the bad guy. In fact I've even got an Academy Award Gnome-ination.
Oh no! This isn't going to be a collection of terrible gnome puns, is it?
Sorry, I just couldn't elf myself.
Yuk! Where do you get all those horrible gags from anyway?
I pixie them up as I go along.
We're surprised you're so keen on jokes — we've always heard that gnomes are extremely short-tempered.
Who are you calling short? Say that again and I'll punch you in the knee.
If you're going to be like that we'll be off.
Suit yourselves – I didn't want to invite you into my toadstool house anyway.
Why not?
Because there's not mushroom inside.

(Interviewer's note: Blimey, he wasn't much of a fun-guy to be with!)

OCCUPATION: FORTUNE-TELLER

Ethel Smith.

What do you mean, 'Ethel Smith'? We haven't asked you a question yet.

I know, but I could foretell that you're going to ask me my name, so I just thought I'd tell you in advance.

Look, there's a proper way to do these interviews, so let's just start from the beginning if it's all right with you. Now, what's your name?

Grizelda Grimaldi.

But you just told us your name was Ethel Smith!

I know – but as well as foreseeing that you were going to ask me my name I also foresaw that you were going to make me tell you my name all over again, so I gave you a false name the first time so as not to spoil the surprise. You're very angry now, aren't you? I can sense it.

Don't tell us if we're angry or not! That's for *us* to decide, not you!!

See? I told you you were very angry.

Don't you realize how irritating it is for other people, guessing what they're going to say all the time?

I knew you were going to ask me that.

ARRGH! That's enough! We've had it! We're out of here!

It's funny, that's how all my interviews end up. People are just so predictable.

Grizelda Grimaldi

VET VERA'S MAGICAL

If you're a wizard or a witch, your pets tend to be a bit more difficult to look after than normal cats and dogs — so it's lucky we've got a vampire vet on hand to answer your queries ... you'd be bats not to listen to her advice.

Dear Vet Vera
During a particularly loud cackling session my familiar, Ferdinand, accidentally hoppe
into my mouth and I swallowed him. What can I do?
Irma Indigestion, Witch

Dear Irma
Try a teaspoon or two of cough medicine. I hear that's a very good cure f
frogs in the throat.

MENAGERIE

Dear Vet Vera
My pet unicorn's horn is broken. What should I do?
Silas Sorcerer

Dear Silas
If his horn's not working, you might like to try giving him a bell or a rattle.

I DON'T MIND BEING VERA'S PET UNICORN BUT I WISH SHE'D FIND SOMEWHERE ELSE TO FILE HER PRESCRIPTIONS!

Dear Vet Vera
I have used my magical powers to create a unique pet of my own design. My pet is two metres tall, is covered in scales at the front, and has hair all over its back. It has huge muscles, long sharp claws, teeth like razors and an extremely bad temper. The only problem is, I'm not sure what to call it. Can you help?
Edward Experimenter, Mad Magician

Dear Edward
If your pet has sharp teeth and claws and a very bad temper, I would call it whatever it wants to be called if I were you.

Dear Vera

I have a pet parrot which is very colourful and exotic-looking. However, whenever I try to do magic at funfairs, local fêtes and other important events, it shouts out things like 'Fake!' and 'It's up his sleeve'. Do you have any suggestions?
Cornelius Conjuror

Dear Cornelius
How about parrot and chips?

Dear Vera

I wrote to you six months ago about the fact that my pet dragon was eating everything in my castle, and so far you haven't bothered to reply.
Amadeus Anxious, Dragon's Keeper

Dear Amadeus
I am sorry it has taken me so long to reply — it took me a long time to work out what you were saying in your letter as your handwriting was very, very bad.

Dear Vera

I would like to see your handwriting after you've been stuck inside a dragon's tummy for the past six months!
Amadeus Evenmore-Anxious, Dragon's Dinner

What do you get if you turn a witch into a parrot?

NOT-VERY-PRETTY POLLY!

I THINK I NEED TO GO AND SEE VET VERA — MY TEMPERATURE ISN'T HIGHER THAN NORMAL!

Dear Vera

It's no wonder you are useless at answering people's pet queries. I happen to know you don't even have a pet yourself!
Glynis GoodyGoody, Fairy

Dear Glynis

Since I am a vampire, I can turn into a bat whenever I want to, so that makes me my own pet. In fact, I think I'll turn into a bat right now and fly over to your place to discuss your letter of complaint in more detail. No need to get in a flap though ... I really like letters I can — heh heh heh — get my teeth into.

Remember, readers — if you have any pet queries, do send them in to Vera ... before Vera comes to visit *you*.

Wizards
v
Witches

Witch: If I was as bad at magic as you, I'd be afraid to show my face.
Wizard: Don't worry — if I had a face like yours, I'd be ashamed to show it too.

Wizard: You look a million dollars.
Witch: Really?
Wizard: Yes, all green and wrinkly.

IT'S NOT BEING
TURNED INTO A FROG
I MIND — IT'S ALL
THE OTHER WIZARDS
SAYING 'I
TOAD YOU
SO!'

Scared of Monsters, Dragons or Mysterious Beasts?
Ward them off with this genuine

LUCKY CHARM

This lucky charm (not shown actual size) is guaranteed to protect you against evil creatures because:

1. It is made by very powerful wizards against whose powers no evil can compete.

2. It is decorated with powerful magic symbols, designed to render any evil attacker powerless.

... but mostly because ...

3. It actually measures two metres in diameter and weighs five tonnes. Simply push it on top of the monster, dragon or mysterious beast of your choice and we promise it will be out of your way in two seconds flat ... and we do mean flat!

BALLOON BRILLIANCE!

Here's a trick that always goes with a bang.

You will need: Two balloons of different colours, a pin

What the magic looks like: This is a good trick to use at the start of your act. You show your audience a large balloon, then you take out a pin and prick it. BANG! Instead of bursting the balloon, you have magically changed it to a different colour!

HERE'S A TRICK I'VE BEEN BURSTING TO SHOW YOU!

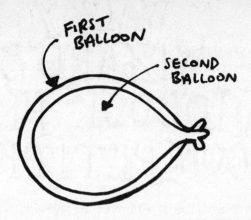

FIRST BALLOON

SECOND BALLOON

How the magic is done: Before you show this trick to your audience, put one balloon inside the other. Now blow up the inside balloon and tie the end. The outside balloon should have stretched to cover the one inside — now carefully blow even more air into the outside balloon so there's a little bit of space between the skin of both balloons, and tie the end. Of course your audience only sees the outside balloon so, as long as you're careful to burst just that one, it will look as if the balloon has changed colour before their very eyes!

OOPS! I TOLD YOU TO BE CAREFUL HOW YOU BLEW UP THOSE BALLOONS!

WACKY WIZARD'S HANDBOOK PRIZE COMPETITION

Simply count the number of wizards on the following two pages and, if you get the number right, you'll win a genuine crock of gold.

Magic Menagerie

Why did the dragon get a traffic fine?
He forgot to put money in the sparking meter.

What did the mummy dragon say to the baby dragon?
'Remember to spark only when you're spoken to.'

WITCH WORKOUT!

Who says witches are wimpier than wizards? Here's a broomstick trick that will sweep those rumours aside!

You will need: Two broomsticks (or brush handles), string

What the magic looks like: With just one piece of string you can pull two broomsticks together, no matter how many people are trying to hold them apart.

"INTERLACE" THE STRING AROUND THE BROOM HANDLES LIKE THIS...

Now the magic is done: As long as you wrap the string around the broom-sticks exactly as shown, this trick will work all by itself ... it's apparently something to do with science and levers and things — but, as you know, we wizards and witches don't understand weird stuff like that!

Mad Magic

What did the policeman say to the three-headed dragon?
Hello, hello, hello.

What do witches' cats read in the morning?
Mewspapers.

If your idea of a fun game with a doll involves sticking lots of pins in it, you'll *love*

BLEARRGHBY

The dress-up witch.

This wonderful witch doll comes complete with her own broomstick and cauldron, and here is even a whole range of lovely clothes to add to your collection. Choose from:

Smelly horrible old rags
Horrible smelly old rags
Old smelly horrible rags

Remember: a Blearrghby may seem expensive, but it's a toy that will last lifetime. (After all, when your little brother pulls *this* doll's head off or your pet cat chews it to ribbons, it can only be an improvement!)

Money-back guarantee: We guarantee to turn you into a frog if you dare ask for your money back!

Magic Menagerie

Did you hear about the wizard who turned himself into a snake?
He hasn't got a leg to stand on.

Did you hear about the wizard who changed himself into a camel?
He's really got the hump.

Why did the wizard bring his bunny to the maths exam?
Because someone told him rabbits multiply rapidly.

What breathes fire and has no legs?
A draggin'.

I HATE HAVING TO PULL A RABBIT OUT OF MY HAT EVERY DAY!

IT'S NOT EVERY DAY – I JUST WANT TO BORROW IT FOR THIS EVENING!

Why do leopards make terrible magicians?
Because, no matter what they try to hide, they're always spotted.

Why did the witch turn her cat into a lemon?
Because he was a sourpuss.

Did you hear about the wizard who turned himself into a wasp?
He got a real buzz out of it.

Did you hear about the wizard who turned himself into a flea?
He had to start again from scratch.

Special Emergency Section!!!!

Ordinary wizards may have amazing powers, but wacky wizards have one amazing power that even they don't have ... the amazing ability to completel[y] muck up even the simplest spell, no matter how hard they practise. That's why we've unearthed th[e] most secret of all forbidden magic books. Trembl[e] now as you read

Ye Secret Booke of Foolproofe Spelles for Really Stupid Sorcerers

Ye Foolproofe Mind-Reading Trick

How it works: The wizard walks on stage and picks a volunteer from the audience, someone he has never met before. He concentrates very hard and is magically able to guess the person's name! Amazing!

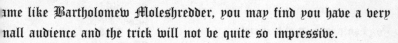

YOUR NAME IS JOHN SMITH!

AND YOUR NAME IS MUD IF ANYONE FINDS OUT HOW THIS TRICK IS DONE!

How it's done: Make sure the tickets to your show are available only to people with the same name. John Smith or Mary Smith are quite good names to pick because, if you decide on a name like Bartholomew Moleshredder, you may find you have a very small audience and the trick will not be quite so impressive.

Special tips: Make sure you remember the name that all the audience members share as otherwise the trick won't work. Actually, if you're desperate enough to be reading this book, you should try hard to remember your own name, as you probably forget that quite often too.

Ye Foolproofe Escape Trick

How it works: The wizard is chained up, tied in a sack and thrown into a deep river, but he manages to escape. Incredible!

How it's done: This trick takes a little time to do, but it is well worth the effort. Once you have been chained up, bagged and thrown into the river, simply wait several centuries and you will find that slowly but surely the chains will rust and the sack will rot away. It will then be a simple matter for you to swim to the surface. Like all wacky wizards, you probably take a bath only once every couple of

THIS TRICK REALLY IS FISHY!

centuries anyway, so this clever trick allows you to kill two birds with one stone.

Special tip: Make sure you get your audience to pay for their tickets in advance since many of them will not be able to wait till the end of the trick (and those who do may well be dead by the time you surface).

Note: Non-wacky wizards may be worried about being able to hold their breath underwater for the required amount of time. Don't worry – when you bathe only once every couple of centuries, you get pretty good at holding your breath!

3. Ye Foolproofe Card Trick

How it works: The wizard asks a volunteer to pick a card, any card. Without looking at the card, the wizard is able to tell that it's the Six of Clubs! Stunning!

I WAS WONDERING HOW THIS TRICK WAS DONE AND THEN IT ~OUCH!'S HIT ME!

WHOP!

How it's done: For this trick you will need an assistant. A suitable assistant would be an ogre, a giant or some other large, tough individual. The evening before the trick is to be done, send your assistant round to the volunteer's house to tell them that unless they pick the Six of Clubs, they will be due for a meeting with the One of Clubs … in other words, the very large club your assistant is holding in his huge hand.

Special tip: Make sure you pay your assistant well for helping with this trick. Otherwise the only card tricks you'll be able to do will be with Get Well Cards.

Ye Foolproofe Vanishing Trick

How it works: The wizard covers a castle with his magic cape, waves his magic wand and – hey presto! – the entire castle disappears. Awesome!

How it's done: Simply make sure that the castle has been filled with dynamite. A couple of sparks from your magic wand should do the rest.

LOOKS LIKE THERE'S BEEN A BIG BOOM IN THE MAGIC BUSINESS!

Special tip: You may have to cough quite loudly to cover the sound of the huge explosion and prevent your audience working out how this trick is done. (On second thoughts, you probably won't have to, since, in addition to making the castle vanish, this trick will also get rid of you, your audience and quite a large part of the surrounding countryside.)

Ye Foolproofe Transformation Trick

How it works: The wizard places a volunteer inside his magic cabinet and, when the cabinet is opened, a cute little puppy dog is in the volunteer's place. Wow! (Not to mention bow wow!)

How it's done: Make sure the volunteer you pick is a werewolf, and perform this trick only when the full moon is about to rise.

HELP! THIS TRICK WASN'T EXACTLY A ROARING SUCCESS!!

Special tips: Special Tip Number One is to make sure to dress the werewolf up in pretty bows and ribbons to get that 'cute puppy' effect. Special Tip Number Two is to RUN! Werewolves don't take kindly to pretty bows and ribbons!

6. Ye Foolproofe Watche Trick

How it works: The wizard borrows a watch from a member of the audience, wraps it in his hanky and breaks it to pieces with a hammer. But then, seconds later, the hanky is unwrapped and the watch reappears – fully restored.

How it's done: Just before you open the hanky, quickly perform a time travel spell which will whisk you, your volunteer and the audience back in time to the point just before you smashed up the watch.

Special Tip Number One: Obviously for this trick to work you'll need to perform the time-travel trick over and over again so you never reveal the smashed-up watch.

Special Tip Number Two: Obviously for this trick to work you'll need to perform the time-travel trick over and over again so you never reveal the smashed-up watch.

Special Tip Number Three: Obviously for this trick to work you'll need to perform the time-travel trick over and over again so ... look, now even a rotten wizard like YOU should have got the idea.

7. Ye Foolproofe Disappearing Trick

How it works: Having amazed audiences up and down the country with wondrous feats like the ones contained in this book, the wacky wizard suddenly and dramatically vanishes, never to be seen again. Phenomenal!

How it's done: Don't worry, it's simple – if you try any of the tricks this book, the Real Wizards Association will be round to your house a flash – and they'll make sure you perfect your disappearing act in n time at all! In fact, you may well vanish for good!

Wizards V Witches

Wizard: I'm nobody's fool.
Witch: Don't worry — I'm sure we can get someone to adopt you!

OUCH! WHEN YOU SAID YOU COULD HANDLE WIZARDS I DIDN'T THINK YOU MEANT WITH A BROOM HANDLE!

Witch: You give me a pain in my head.
Wizard: That must be the first thing you've had inside your head for ages.

BIZARRE

Why settle for a boring old magic book when you can have a book that actually does magic all by itself?

You will need: A hardback book, paper clips

What the magic looks like: You put some paper clips on top of your open magic book and then shake them off on to the table. Suddenly there are a lot more paper clips.

SMALL NUMBER OF CLIPS

THIS TRICK WILL REALLY SHAKE 'EM UP!

LOTS OF CLIPS!

BOOK

HIDE THE EXTRA CLIPS IN THE SPINE OF THE BOOK.

MAGIC

How the magic is done: For this trick you need an old-fashioned hardback book ... one with a small gap between the cover and the spine of the book. Paperback books like this one and many modern hardback books have their pages tightly bound or glued together, so there isn't a space; but you should find that one of the older books from your library will fit the bill. Old books look more magical anyway — in fact, you could even make a magical cover to fold over the book. (We know you'd never actually write on the book itself, of course!)

Before you do the trick, all you have to do is hide a few extra paper clips inside the spine of the book. When the book is shut, they'll be held tightly inside, and you should be able to open the book without tipping them out until it's time for them to fall out with the others. Coloured paper clips look even more impressive, or you could try paper stars ... in fact, you could write a book about all the things you can magically multiply with this trick, once you know the secret!

Wizard School Wackiness

Wizard Pupil: Teacher, Teacher — this witch sitting beside me is preventing me from doing my exam.

Wizard Teacher: Why? What is she doing?

Wizard Pupil: She's covering her answers before I can copy them down!

What has eight legs, eight eyes and four long white beards?
The front row of a Wizard School classroom.

Wizard Teacher: What can you tell me about the birth of Merlin the Magician?

Wizard Pupil: That it happened when he was very young?

WHERE DO WIZARDS STAY DURING THEIR HOLIDAYS?

AT A MERL-INN!

Wizard Teacher: Why haven't you got your homework done?

Trainee Witch: Because I cleaned out my cauldron yesterday.

Wizard Teacher: How would that stop you doing your homework?

Trainee Witch: Haven't you heard that a washed pot never boils?

Are you tired of breakfasts that just go snap, crackle or pop?

Try

COSMIC CRISPIES

the cereal that goes snap, crackle, pop, whizz, fizz, zap and ka-boom*

*This is because Cosmic Crispies are full of raw magic, so don't blame us if you turn into a spotted warthog first thing in the morning

Wizard Wit

Did you hear about the wizard who accidentally turned himself into a fly?
He ended up in the soup.

Did you hear about the wizard who turned himself into a pot of glue?
He came to a sticky end.

Revise for your History exams in a flash with our guide to:

MAGIC THROUGH THE AGES

Stone Age

Egyptian

Viking

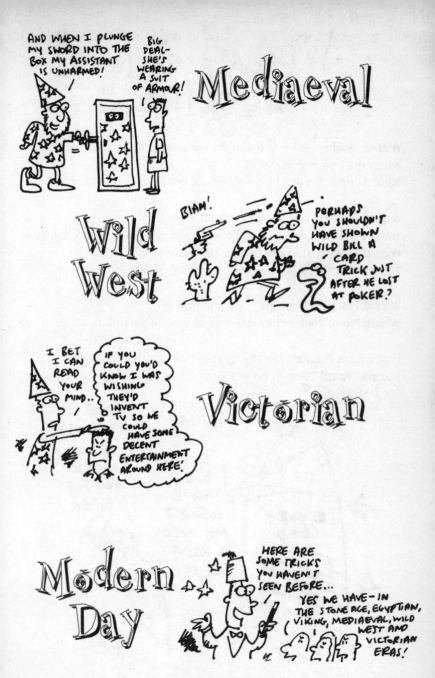

Wizard School Wackiness

Wizard Teacher: Put that magic mirror away! You've been looking at yourself all through class!
Wizard Pupil: But you told me I should watch my behaviour!

Wizard Teacher: Why are you late for school?
Trainee Witch: I dreamt I was cooking a magic potion in my cauldron.
Wizard Teacher: How did that make you late?
Trainee Witch: Everyone wanted second helpings.

Wizard Teacher: What spells are you best at?
Wizard Pupil: Well, I often get a good spell in detention.

First Wizard Teacher: Are any of your class good at magic?
Second Wizard Teacher: Oh yes — in fact, when they get something right it's a miracle!

Wizard Pupil: Help! I've accidentally made my legs vanish!
Wizard Teacher: I told you not to try that spell, so don't come running to me!

Wizard Teacher: Why have you turned the classroom clock into a football?
Wizard Pupil: I was hoping it would pass the time.

Wizard Teacher: Why are you late for school? Your candy cottage is just around the corner.
Trainee Witch: I know, but it takes me two hours to get out of the wrapper.

Wizard Teacher: Why are you rolling that crystal ball around the classroom?
Wizard Pupil: I'm really sorry, sir — I must have lost my marbles!

Every wizard knows that midnight is the ideal time for casting spells and doing magical deeds. But even for wizards it's hard to get all your work done in such a short space of time. That's why you need the new

WIZWATCH

With twelve midnights every day you've got all the time you need.

Crime warning: We have had reports of several Wizwatch thefts by gangs of vampires who seem to like the idea of it being midnight all the time. If you spot a vampire lurking around your area, don't forget to put your Wizwatch forward so that it's twelve noon all the time. Then we guarantee you won't see the vampire for dust.

Magical dictionary
(aka - Words of Wiz-dom!)

Astrology — the study of fortune-telling by star signs

Ass-trology — the study of the kind of person who believes you can tell your fortune by reading star signs

Broomstick — the kind of glue witches use to repair broken brooms

Card tricks — any magic that involves ribbons, rings and pieces of rope. (OK, OK — we *know* those things have nothing to do with cards, but you wanted a trick, didn't you?)

Clairvoyant — a woman called Clair who can see into the future

Clairviolent — what Clair got when she saw our definition of Ass-trology

Conjuror — someone on a jury who isn't very honest

Dragon — what your feet are doing when you're on the way to school on Monday morning

Fairy godmother — a kind old lady (see also **Hairy godmother** — a kind old lady who also happens to be a werewolf)

Familiar — a pet for a wizard or a witch (see also **Unfamiliar** — a pet for a wizard or a witch with a really bad memory)

Full moon — a moon that's eaten too much

Ghost — a pale, scary spirit (or a tanned, scary spirit — all depends on whether it comes from the West Ghost or the East Ghost)

Lucky charm — a piece of jewellery, designed to bring you good luck, which you wear around your neck or hide in your pocket

WE'VE TURNED OURSELVES INTO LETTERS!

FOR ONCE YOU MIGHT BE GOOD AT SPELLING!

(see also **Unlucky charm** — a piece of jewellery, designed to bring you good luck, but which actually brings your neck out in a rash or tears a hole in your pocket)

Magic circle — a collection of magicians

Magic square — a collection of magicians who don't dress very trendily

Magic triangle — a place in Bermuda that magicians never seem to come back from

Palm reading — the study of fortune-telling using large green plants

Frogs — small green reptiles (yes, we know Frog doesn't begin with P, but this frog is really a prince!)

Spelling — what wizards learn at Wizard School

(see also **Zkool** — how wizards spell 'school' if they don't pay attention to their spelling)

Tea-leaves — some wizards believe you can read messages in these

Tea-shirt — even more wizards believe you can read messages on these, such as what football team someone supports or who your favourite pop group

Tea-break — what football hooligans do to the necks of wizards when they find them sticking their noses in their tea or staring at their tea-shirts

Hi! I'm a MAGIC 'R'.

You've come too early in the alphabet! Get to the end of the 'Q'!

Hi - I'm a MAGIC 'Z' you'll find me and lots of my friends in the audience at a WACKY WIZARDS show...

SNORE! SNORE!

Trick questions — the only sort of questions contained in Wizard School exam papers

Vampire — how much it costs to hire a vamp

Voodoo — what you find in the nappy of a baby voo

Witchcraft — like a spacecraft, only full of witches

Wizard of Oz — someone who lives in the Emerald City, holds lots of barbecues and never misses 'Neighbours'.